The
JOURNEY
of
TRANSFORMATION

The JOURNEY *of* TRANSFORMATION

Six Essential Steps to Achieving
Your Goal of Change

D. F. PEN

CONSORTIUM

NEW YORK

Published by

Consortium Press, New York

The Journey of Transformation

ISBN: 978-1-7322136-0-9

Book Design by AuthorSupport.com

Printed in the United States of America

Contents

To those who have decided that the time for change is now, remember that when you make a decision, all the forces of the universe are prepared to support your intentions. It is your action, however, that will render the experience. This is not simply *"a"* journey of transformation; this is *"YOUR"* journey of transformation. Congratulations on your decision to begin today.

*"The journey of Transformation begins with
a seed planted in the heart of man."*

A Note to the Reader

Congratulations on your decision to embark on your personal journey of transformation.

Please be reminded that a journey does not have to take a very long time—especially this one, because it is intimately personal. Your journey will take as long as necessary to achieve your objective of change.

ABOUT THIS BOOK:

As you make your way through the pages, each section will begin with a "Thinking on Paper" reflection prompt, which contains a question, series of questions, or reflective activity.

Feel free to write in this book, or use a separate notepad or computer program, etc., to record your information. These questions and activities are the elements that personalize the journey, and will also allow you to go back and analyze the steps in this process as you progress to your goal.

As you engage in the process, these questions and activities become the focus of the book. Your involvement by way of your honesty, critical analysis, and intentional reflection will prove to be very influential on what you get out of it.

Consider this book only partly written and awaiting the contribution from the ink of your pen.

Consider these three phases of progression:

Phase I
The Read through
This phase is for *Information*

Phase II
The Work through
This Phase is for *Application*

Phase III
The Reflection
This Phase is for *Evaluation*

Remember, "It is the process that produces results..."
Again, congratulations; and welcome to your journey!

Introduction

Personal transformation is first an idea conceived in the heart of an individual. This idea is like a seed that has an insatiable desire to blossom and display its beauty to the world. The idea, once conceived, is then initiated by action and nurtured to fulfillment by dedication and commitment. Quitting is not even a consideration, because the flower of achievement is more desirable than the seed of potential. What an exhilarating feeling, to experience a personal transformation! In a reflective moment, it is easy to acknowledge and attest that we all have gone through and will go through many changes during life's journey. These changes can be mental, emotional, physical, social, financial—the list goes on. For the most part, as it is understood, change is necessary and therefore can be expected.

In your time of reflection, take a moment to acknowledge the very important changes that have occurred in your life. As you engage in this mental activity, be sure to take notice of the subtle changes that may have been small and less spectacular, but very impactful nonetheless. They are the little changes that you would not even acknowledge unless they were brought to your attention. These little changes could be responsible for keeping you on track to your goals or preventing disaster in your life. When looking back and reflecting, give yourself credit and be very thankful. In many cases, the actual change itself is what you remember, because it represents the outcome or the accomplishment, the new state, or the goal attained; however, the most important component is often overlooked. Transformative change is not so much about the outcome as it is the process. The process is where the major transformation takes place, because it is in the many little changes, adjustments, and decisions along the way that the final transformation becomes possible. The process of transformation is the arena where the real learning and development takes place. It is in the process where true discipline and commitment are tested. It is in the process where fortitude and resilience are challenged, and how you respond in the face of these challenges, tests, and distractions will determine your progression and advancement toward your pre-established objectives.

It has been often stated that when a person wants something bad enough, they tend to get it. They dismiss the notion that any obstacle or challenge will be able to stop them. They predetermine that they will do whatever it takes, and they become unstoppable and relentless. So the question is, why are there only a few occasions that we have this experience, and what provokes such an intense desire? What drives us to the point where we determine a change is necessary, and that we will no longer accept or tolerate the way things are? What is the spark that ignites the fire inside of us that causes us to say, "I am ready and willing to do whatever it takes, because this change is necessary"?

To always be intending to live a new life, but never find time to set about it—this is as if a man should put off eating and drinking from one day to another till he be starved and destroyed.

—WALTER SCOTT

Identifying the Spark

THINKING ON PAPER

Identify what has led and inspired you to arrive at the conclusion that it is time for a change.

_____

_____

_____

_____

_____

What is the change you desire?
- First, identify the current state or condition.

_____

_____

_____

_____

_____

- Second, state specifically the desired state or condition you would like to experience.

_____

_____

_____

_____

_____

On a scale of 1–10, rank how important this desired change is to you (with 1 being the lowest and 10 being the highest).

Ranking: _____

Identify three action items you are considering taking to achieve this objective.

Action Item #1

_____

_____

_____

_____

_____

Action Item #2

_____

_____

_____

_____

_____

Action Item #3

_____

_____

_____

_____

_____

SAMPLE

Identify what has led and inspired you to arrive at the conclusion that it is time for a change.

> While attending my daughter's dance recital, I realized that I have missed the majority of the things that she is involved in ever since I got promoted four years ago. She is 11 years old now, and I have not been there for the things that matter to her. I realize that if this continues, I will have missed the majority of her childhood experiences, which I will never get back. This cannot and will not continue. It is time for a change.

State specifically the change you desire.

- First, identify the current state or condition.

> Currently, I am a working husband and father who has experienced a level of success both professionally and financially. Unfortunately, this "success" seems to have a hidden cost that I did not realize: my time. I am usually working late, and, often on weekends. This time constraint has caused me to be absent from my daughter's life. In addition, I know my wife is also experiencing the strain as well as the absence of her husband. After taking inventory, I realize that I am working during what should be family time. Basically, I am not with my family enough and I am at work too much.

- Second, state specifically the desired state or condition you would like to experience.

The desired state I will achieve is to be there more for my family. I will be home in the evenings to have dinner with them, watch a movie, and be at any evening activities my daughter may have (even if it is simply driving her to practice). I will be around on weekends to simply hang out and enjoy the people I love. I will no longer work late hours at the expense of time with them. If I work late, it will be only if there is nothing going on, and this occurrence will be limited to one time per month (if that). I plan on being home for dinner and even cooking dinner; or, if we feel up to it, we will go out to dinner as a family. The change I will achieve is going from not being a family man to being a family man. My daughter and wife mean the world to me.

On a scale of 1–10, rank how important this desired change is to you (with 1 being the lowest and 10 being the highest).

Ranking: 10

Identify three action items you are considering taking to achieve this objective.

Action Item #1

Set up a meeting with the partners to discuss my responsibilities and new time commitments I am able to fulfill. If necessary, entertain the conversation and consideration of a different role and possible pay adjustment. The time commitment, unfortunately, will be nonnegotiable, because I have sacrificed enough these past four years. I owe it to my family to not permit the neglect to continue.

Action Item #2

Plan a family vacation for this year.

Action Item #3

Get my daughter's schedules and block out those time slots on my calendar, so I can be at every event.

STEP 1

Identifying the Spark

Don't be fooled by the calendar. There are only as many days in the year as you make use of.

—CHARLES RICHARDS

What brings a person to the point of determining that it is time for a change?

SEVEN CONSIDERATIONS:

1. A Major Life Event

For example:

- the birth of your first child (or expecting your first child)
- securing employment in the career you desired
- earning the promotion you always wanted
- making the decision to get married, separated, or divorced
- graduating from high school, college, and so on
- going to or returning from military duty

2. *Disaster*

For example:

- being fired, released, or laid off from your job or company, resulting in the loss of a major income stream
- losing a major client or contributor in business
- being abruptly separated from your family
- a major loss, such as the dissolving of a major relationship that you have grown accustomed to being in

3. *Reflection*

For example:

- realizing or acknowledging that where you are at is not where you should be (the prodigal daughter or son experience)
- coming to terms that you really want more from life, because you realize that you have settled and you know you deserve better
- wanting to be more than you have become, because you realize that complacency has stunted your growth and stifled your motivation to pursue the desires of your heart

4. Frustration

For example:

- becoming tired of the way things are and knowing that you have to do something now or things will never change
- realizing that you have tolerated an undesired condition long enough and finally acknowledging that it is hindering other areas of your life (the displacement effect)

5. Exposure

For example:

- getting a taste of something different which ignites a desire for something new
- having your eyes opened to the reality that there is more to life than your limited experience

6. Fear

For example:

- knowing and recognizing that if you do not do something now something very bad is on the horizon
- the doctor telling you to lose weight or you will soon die of a heart attack
- escaping death when you know you should have died (the grace experience)
- seeing someone close to you reaping the undesired fruits of their deeds
- preparing for the unknown (e.g., being deployed, moving out, finally leaving what you have been comfortable in for a while, and so on)

7. A Burning Desire

For example:

- arriving at a point where that burning desire that was born on the inside refuses to be quenched and fuels the heart to do something now

Establish Your Compelling "Why"

THINKING ON PAPER

Why is this change important to you?

This change is important to me because...
_____
_____
_____
_____
_____
_____
_____
_____
_____
_____
_____
_____
_____
_____

STEP 2

Establish Your Compelling "Why"

Don't quit. Never give up trying to build the world you can see, even if others can't see it. Listen to your drum and your drum only. It's the one that makes the sweetest sound.

—**SIMON SINEK**

Congratulations on your decision to embark on the journey of transformation. After deliberately thinking about it and preparing to take action, you should now have a clear description of what your transformation will look like once you have achieved it. This description should be committed to paper. The exercise of writing out your vision of transformation can be an exciting task, as you begin to describe what you would like to see as your transformative change. When you are writing it down, what you are also doing is engaging your mental imagery. The imagination is what adds color to our black-and-white thoughts. As you engage in this process, you begin to get a clearer picture of what this transformation will look like. The process of engaging the imagination is like viewing your vision with special 3-D glasses. The more you engage your imagination in this process, the more real the vision appears. At some point, it should feel like you can almost reach out and touch it, and with persistence and diligence, in time you will.

Let's refer to the analogy of the caterpillar and the butterfly that is often used when illustrating this phenomenon of transformation. When you hear the word "butterfly," a visual image of a butterfly appears. Depending on your exposure to the species, you may have different pictures of what a butterfly looks like; however, what you visualize is something that is distinctly different from a caterpillar. In seeing this butterfly and the beauty you may acknowledge it to possess, you simultaneously also acknowledge the fact that it is no longer what it used to be. You may even find it difficult to imagine that it was ever anything else. Just think of how insignificant you make the caterpillar as you acknowledge the butterfly! Rarely does one acknowledge that if it were not for the caterpillar, the butterfly would not exist. The reality is that the old is often forgotten when the new is being celebrated.

When you begin to consider yourself and the transformation that will soon occur, your current state will become a distant memory as your new self takes permanent residence. Therefore, take the time to write the vision, and draw a clear and vivid picture on both your mental and physical canvases so that your pursuit can be precise and your focus can be clear.

THE NEXT STEP

This next step is going to be one of the utmost importance, and that is starting with a compelling "why." This thought, which was inspired by a TED Talk presented by Simon Sinek, reflects a basic tenet of human initiative and sustained motivational drive.

When you have started to consider pursuing the goal of transformative change, the most critical question to ask yourself is "Why?" Why do you want to experience this transformative change in your life? Sadly, most people will never take themselves seriously, because their "why" is not even convincing to them. To simply say "I would like to live a healthier lifestyle, because that is what my friends are doing" may get you started, but lacks the depth of conviction to compel you to continue. The question is not why your friends want to do it, but why you want to do it. Your "why" must be compelling to you, because in the face of mental, physical, and emotional fatigue, it must fuel your drive to continue.

Consider the purchase of a brand-new laser printer. With your purchase, the manufacturer often provides you with a starter toner supply. This will allow you to get started using your printer immediately; however, it is intended to be temporary. As you use your printer, the documents look pristine, and you are so excited with your new purchase that you never bother to think long-term and make the purchase of the additional toner that is designed for full operation. Then, as you are enjoying using your printer, you see that the print quality quickly decreases and the documents are faded. Within no time, the toner is completely empty and you are unable to print. Sadly, it seems that the printer has no consideration for the importance of the documents you need to print. You take the toner bottle out and shake it, but your efforts are in vain. You realize that the initial use was all you had enough toner for.

Your "why" has to be like that new bottle of toner: prepared for the long-term, sufficient to take on the big job, and able to promote sustainability. Your "why" should be that motivational factor that allows you to continue even when that initial burst of enthusiasm begins to fade. Your "why" must be convincing and compelling enough for you to anchor yourself during the turbulence of the transition. During the process of transformation, you may reach a point where the excitement has dimmed and the novelty of the new thing you're doing has fully faded. The process may become mundane, and continuing becomes more challenging and less desirable. Your "why" must be the fire that fuels your motivation for continued and sustained action. Your "why" must be the voice on the inside that refuses to consider quitting, and reminds you of the importance and necessity of completing your journey of transformation.

Remember, your "why" must compel you. Avoid the

common mistake that many make, which is attempting to compel or convince others. Please be warned that you should refrain from galvanizing and directing your energy in trying to convince others. Maintain a deliberate focus on convincing yourself, because it will be you, not them, who is responsible for action.

To Convince

Let's take a moment to examine a different perspective on the word "convince". As we dissect the term, be mindful to remember the context of establishing a compelling "why" is for the purpose of pursuing transformative change. Now, when we start to look at this word, "convince," let's parallel it with the term "convict." When you have to convince yourself to do something that is important, you must have conviction. This conviction will become critical, and it actually has two distinctions. First, conviction is a necessity for sustained action. Conviction fuels action. When people have conviction, they often tend to act. When you consider the idea of conviction in the sense of intense passion and fervor, the mental imagery may be of someone who displays religious conviction. Their religious conviction is often displayed in the actions that they take. When someone has religious conviction, you may find that they are more than likely beyond the point of being able to be persuaded to believe or act in a manner contrary to their conviction. There is a conviction within them that promotes action. So when you are convincing yourself, you must have a similar conviction. This conviction will be the fuel that motivates and sustains action, because it is ignited and burns from the inside.

The second element of conviction is actually the ability to convict. When you have true conviction, it has the ability to confer upon you a sense of guilt and disappointment. When you experience this inner conviction regarding a particular action or inaction, you may feel a sense of guilt. When a person is truly convicted for underachieving, they feel a sense of disappointment. Therefore, when you consider the potential to guide and direct your actions, this type of conviction can actually be very healthy. Consider the referee that blows the whistle when you step out of bounds, or issues a penalty for deviating from the rules of participation in a particular event. He blows the whistle to inform you that you have violated the rule, and penalizes you to discourage repeated behavior. When you fall short and you are convicted, it is perfectly fine that you should feel a sense of guilt and disappointment. When straying from your pre-established goal of change, it is okay if you feel as if you underachieved, because you did. When you fall short, this conviction is a signal that your effort is unacceptable, and that you are better than the effort you are displaying. This conviction is telling you that what you are doing is not in alignment with your goal of transformation. You should not shy away from conviction, but embrace its natural and pure intention to discourage behaviors that are counterproductive to your goals.

Now, the real problem is when you fall short and you become okay with it. We live in a society where everything is expected to turn out okay despite effort. Very few people acknowledge failure, and many are convinced that in some way, they have succeeded regardless of contradicting outcomes. Disappointment is avoided by false perceptions of succeeding, and justifications for failure seem to be readily available, with no shortage in supply. Despite this avoidance behavior, the reality is that when it relates to transformative change, the outcome is what is experienced. Therefore, if the outcome has not been achieved, then you have fallen short. If you set out to, let's say, live a healthier lifestyle, and you have identified actions that would align with this healthier lifestyle, and then you stray from these pre-established actions, then what true conviction should do is cause you to feel a sense of guilt or disappointment for straying. Basically, conviction should prod you to get back on track, rather than cosign your rationale or excuse for deviating.

If failure becomes acceptable, then it becomes frequent.

Again, the problem arises when you fall short and you become okay with it. This mindset ultimately permits failure to become acceptable, and consequently promotes its frequency. When failure becomes frequent, then it becomes the norm. When failure becomes the norm, then success becomes abnormal. Once success becomes abnormal, then success moves from a realistic aspiration to being dismissed as a lofty fantasy, unattainable with any amount of effort; so now your goal of transformative change, which was once a realistic aspiration that you were going to make strides toward achieving, becomes the object of resentment and counterproductive actions.

When failure becomes the norm, the very sight of success provokes the default action of self-sabotage. Once failure has become accepted, frequent, and normative, it is solidified as the status quo in your life. Straying from your goals and not exercising discipline becomes the status quo. Once you become okay with it, there is no conviction when you do it. It's almost like becoming callous to the fact that you have fallen short. Once this occurs, we find that success is going to be positioned as antagonistic to your established status quo of failure. As contradictory as it may sound, self-sabotage is an unconscious protective action deliberately attempting to protect the status quo of failure. Consequently, you will see failure perpetuated rather than success promoted.

The unconscious protection of this counterproductive status quo or norm of failure becomes like the cement that will bind one's feet to the platform of mediocrity. Sadly, you will be stuck there, because you have accepted failure. Conviction, as we can see, is actually not just nice to have, but a critical component. When you are convicted of straying or falling short, the feeling of disappointment—and even shame—should promote you to declare, "This is not what I am supposed to be doing. This is not what my goal is. I need to move forward, I need to pick myself up, and I need to exercise resilience to get back in the game." Then act in accordance with your goals.

This is a likely challenge that you may experience on your journey to transformation; however, always remember that your failure is something that does not have to be final. It is just an indication that you have fallen short of your predetermined objectives. Conviction should serve as a motivating factor that you should get back on track.

When you begin to establish your "why," remember that it must have the ability to convince you, and it also must have the ability to convict you. This conviction has two main responsibilities that you must embrace and be conscious of: First, is its ability to motivate you to act, and second, its ability to encourage you to wave the red flag when you have strayed. Your goals are important, and it is unacceptable for you to accept a mediocre or substandard effort from yourself. If this occurs, acknowledge the shortcoming, accept full responsibility, and readjust to act in alignment with your goals.

Again, it is of the utmost importance to establish your compelling "why," and determine whether it possesses the ability to convince as well as convict you, allowing it to serve as the fire that will continue to fuel your motivation for progressive action.

> *Whatever you can do or dream you can, begin it.*
> *Boldness has genius, power, and magic in it.*

JOHANN WOLFGANG VON GOETHE

Take the Leap,
Then Start Stepping

THINKING ON PAPER

Do Something Drastic

Referring back to your anticipated action items, select the one that you believe would be considered a "leap" (the action that establishes your commitment). What do you plan on doing that will not only get your attention and prove that you are serious, but also surprise the hell out of you?

If none of them fall into this category, draft a new "leap" action now. Again, this action establishes your commitment.

Explain how this action is relevant to propelling you to get moving toward the pursuit of the change you desire.

_____

_____

_____

_____

_____

_____

_____

_____

_____

_____

_____

_____

_____

_____

_____

_____

After identifying your "leap," list as many steps as possible that will follow this initial commitment. (These are the steps that answer the question "I took the leap, now what?") These steps should be as detailed as possible, so that there are no delays or lapses in time following your "leap." Harnessing this momentum is very important.

1. _____
   _____
   _____

2. _____
   _____
   _____

3. _____
   _____
   _____

4. _____
   _____
   _____

5. _____
   _____
   _____

6. _____

_____

_____

7. _____

_____

_____

STEP 3

Take the Leap,
Then Start Stepping

Why live on the edge when you can jump off it?

—SIGN AT MACAU TOWER BUNGEE JUMP

You may have often heard that "the journey of a thousand miles begins with a single step." That may be true in some cases; however, this journey will not begin with a single step, but with a great leap. This great leap is deliberate and is going to force you to make that initial commitment.

DO SOMETHING DRASTIC

In a noisy world, the voice that whispers is only heard in complete silence, and despite the significance of the match; it is the fireworks that get the attention of the people. When embarking on the journey of transformative change, the first challenge that you have to confront is the fact that you are probably not going to take yourself seriously.

Therefore, you will have to do something drastic to get your own attention. As children, we all may have encountered a threat from our parents that we did not believe; use your imagination for a moment to illustrate this point. The teenager is sitting on the couch watching their favorite show and communicating on the phone with their friend. The parent has requested more than once that the garbage needs to be taken out—now. The fact that the child still remains on the couch leads one to draw one of two conclusions: The child is either deaf or disobedient.

Well, consider the hypothetical scenario: The parent returns and threatens, "If you do not get the garbage out right now, I am going to smash that phone and the television." Minutes later, the child is unmoved. The parent returns with a sledgehammer, approaches the television, and smashes it several times. Then the parent grabs the child's phone and stomps on it until it is in pieces. As you can imagine, the child is on their feet screaming, "What are you doing?"

We can agree this is most likely a rhetorical question, as the child is watching in utter astonishment. The parent is doing exactly what they articulated they would do if the garbage was not taken out. With the sledgehammer in hand, sweating and breathing heavily, the parent simply stares at the child and does not utter a word. Shocked, scared, and unsure, the child runs into the kitchen, grabs the garbage, takes it out immediately, and runs upstairs to their room and locks the door. In short, the parent got the child's attention, and the child now knows that the parent is serious. When beginning this journey of transformation, you will need to take yourself seriously, and in order to do that, you will need to do something that shocks you and arrests your attention. This drastic move will serve as a sign to yourself and others that this is not all talk: "I really mean it this time."

MAKE THE COMMITMENT EASY

Consider the skydiving decision. All of the contemplation and deliberation is over when you make the move and jump. "Should I jump?" is no longer a consideration, and you do not have to decide on the way down whether you want to go through with your decision. The entire world changes because now there is a different focus. The only thing that is of real significance is enjoying the dive and landing without serious injury. When you jump, the decision is made at the time of departing from that open door, and your commitment is irreversible because there is no returning to that plane. Again, when you are beginning the process of transformative change, it is essential to do something drastic that gets your own attention and ensures your initial commitment, because quitting, regressing, or backing out are no longer options. The new mindset is to honor your commitment to the change you desire. In many cases, you may be so shocked at your initial action that you may need a minute to process what you have done. You may say, "Oh my goodness, I can't believe I just did that!"

Unfortunately, this is not the time to sit back and reflect on your action, because the initial act is a sign that the game is on, and there is no turning back now.

As you know, the term "drastic" is subjective based on your definition. However, it is important to be sure to be honest with yourself. Let's use the classic example of smoking. The anticipated transformation may sound like, "I want to go from being a smoker to being a nonsmoker." The common thought is that it's going to be a process. You are going to have to go through certain prerequisites, and then, eventually, you will stop. Maybe if you smoke two packs a day, you go down to a pack and a half; this first step may be viewed as an accomplishment and is often celebrated, allowing you to feel good. But a first leap may look a little different. You might decide, "I am going to take every cigarette that I own (even the hidden ones) and crush them to pieces. Then I am going to burn them in the yard." (Be sure it is the front yard, so that when the neighbors inquire, you are forced to disclose that you have quit smoking.)

Consider the person desiring to drop a few sizes and adopt a healthier lifestyle. They may take all of their clothes except for three ensembles and donate them to charity. Then they open the cabinets and refrigerator, and give everything in them to the local soup kitchen. Why? Because with empty cabinets and refrigerator, the only items that should refill them are foods consistent with the new lifestyle that has been chosen. This initial change must be drastic, and it must be visible. A classic example is the bald head. When this occurs, the initial encounter with those who know you usually begins with the acknowledgment, "Oh my goodness, you cut off all your hair!" In response, you may answer, "Yes; this is the new me now." Such a response usually provokes a follow-up question like, "So, why did you do that?" This is an easy answer, because before you acted, you established a compelling and convincing why.

So this drastic act is something that has to get your attention; but it is also something that has to provoke inquiry by those that recognize that something is different. A friend or family member may ask, "I notice you have been wearing that same outfit for the last two weeks. Is everything okay?" That gives you the opportunity to reply, "Yes, I have seven more pounds to lose before I can fit into the new size that I desire." When you commit to do something drastic, there is no turning back.

Have a Plan for When You Land

A "leap" is an action that clearly says "I started, and I have made a commitment." The same leap applies in the context of any transformative change you desire to pursue. Force yourself to take the leap first; and then when you land, start stepping.

If you reflect back over your life, you have already taken many leaps. In the process of transformative change, it will be critical to clearly define the necessary steps in the process.

After the leap has been made and you have landed, you must know the next series of steps in your strides toward your transformation.

Many people say "Take a leap of faith." However, transformative change is going to be the result of the progressive and consistent steps toward the goal. Big changes are the result of an accumulation of very small steps. Transformation is the destination of these steps, indicating that "This was what used to be, and this is what is now.

Action provokes inquiry, and inquiry provokes
involvement, and involvement sustains movement, and
movement maintains momentum, and momentum
creates force, and force creates change...

- UNKNOWN

BE PREPARED TO CONFRONT FEAR

This journey will rest on your ability to recognize and confront fear. When you are considering taking a leap, the biggest challenge you will face is fear. As humans, we tend to fear the unknown. The transformation is a journey into the unknown. Taking a leap is one of the scariest things you can do. Just consider jumping into a body of water that you believe may contain alligators; despite you never having seen an alligator in the water, your mind can begin to play a horror scene that even the greatest cinematographers could only dream of replicating. This fear causes the paralysis that keeps people on the banks of life, rather than swimming in the ocean of opportunity. Jumping in becomes an impossibility, and even the consideration of getting close to the water causes your heart to race. Regardless of how much you want to get in the water, the only way in is to jump. When you really consider the fear, it was never of the water, but of the unknown of what may lie beneath. It was your imagination that made the undesired outcome so real that you may even recall seeing an alligator that never existed. When you take a leap, you make an internal decision to deal with whatever comes, whenever it comes. Taking a leap is confronting your fear head on, which is actually a huge step. As you know, when you leap, there is no turning back; you become like the Spanish explorer Cortez, who was said to have burned his ships, leaving himself and his men no option to retreat. Once the ships are burned, then the fight begins—and that is to complete the mission. The intentional leap differs greatly from the casual leap. Consider the person who decides to go skydiving; this person leaps from the plane and enjoys an exhilarating experience, with the only major objective being to land safely. Take the Navy SEAL, on the other hand, and consider the difference when he jumps. Prior to jumping, there is a very detailed and specific plan of action directing the steps immediately following the moment his feet hit the ground. This plan is critical to the mission. When you take your leap, it is to establish your commitment. Be sure to have your plan before you jump, so that when you land, you immediately get to stepping toward the mission of transformative change. Take the leap, and then start stepping.

> *Twenty years from now you will be more disappointed by the things you didn't do than by the ones you did. So throw off the bowlines, sail away from the safe harbor, catch the trade winds in your sails. Explore. Dream. Discover.*

> **- MARK TWAIN**

Pay Money for Something: Get Invested

THINKING ON PAPER

What will you pay for that represents your financial commitment to achieving your desired change?

_____

_____

_____

_____

_____

_____

_____

Explain why this purchase or investment and the cost
are significant.

_____

_____

_____

_____

_____

_____

_____

_____

_____

_____

_____

STEP 4

Pay Money for Something: Get Invested

For where your treasure is, there your heart will be also.

Matthew 6:21(KJV)

In today's society, it's very interesting to see what money has evolved to represent. When you consider its worth, money does not simply reflect the numeric value it has been assigned, but the time, energy, and effort that someone has committed to obtaining it. This is very important, because it is a great leveraging tool. When you pay for or commit monetary resources to something, you acknowledge there is an investment that you are making. Concerning the process of transformative change, you absolutely want to put yourself in a position to say, "I have made a monetary investment. My time, my energy, and the effort that I have exchanged to receive this money will now be invested into something that will assist me in achieving the transformation that I desire." Never bargain-shop or be frugal in this practice. Seek out and secure the very best your money can buy. What you expect from it should be consistent with what you have invested into it. In short, it should cost you enough that you are constantly reminded that you paid "good" money for it.

Let's use the classic example of living a healthier lifestyle. You may hear yourself say, "I am going to start going to the gym. I am going to start eating healthfully. I am going to start jogging in the morning." These plans and thoughts are great; however, they lack the investment that triggers the loss-aversion behavioral motivation initiative which propels one to act to prevent real or perceived potential loss. What did you pay for, and what do you fear losing? Go ahead and purchase all-new, expensive training gear. Why? Because you know how much hard-earned money was spent on purchasing this gear, you are probably going to be less inclined to let it sit folded neatly in the trunk of your car. You are less likely to prepare your expensive gym bag with your expensive training gear and never to go to the gym that you paid an expensive membership fee for. Again, the word "expensive" is subjective; therefore, be intentional and make the cost significant.

Once again, let's refer back to healthy eating and food choices to achieve personal fitness goals. At the beginning, you may consider forgoing an attempt at shopping and only purchase from the produce and organic aisles. Start off by paying for Weight Watchers, or hiring a personal chef recommended by a nutritionist. Yes, you might be able to do it yourself at home, but choose to pay. Why? Because now, the monetary value is not in the meal preparation or the personal chef or Weight Watchers, but in the fact that it took your time, energy, and effort to earn that money. The act of allocating those funds for these goods or services means you are invested in the transformation that you desire. Go ahead; buy yourself a $500 blender. Why? Because it forces you to say, "Now I am financially committed, because I refuse to let this blender sit on the counter." And if you do let it sit on the counter, return it and purchase the one for $900.

The financial commitment is usually a good motivation for many people, because they will often function under the economic concept of utility maximization and say, "I have to get my money's worth." So, go ahead and buy a gym membership. Why? Because you know if you buy a gym membership, you will not want it go to waste; you may go to the gym and run on the treadmill for an hour just because you want to feel like you are getting some use out of that membership. If you find yourself staying home, cancel that membership, pay the fee to break your contract, and sign up with a more expensive gym. It may sound ridiculous, but you must get invested financially and motivated by any means necessary. Yes: Put your money where your mouth is. Be sure to consider the mindset of an investor. The objective is not to simply have an expense, but to invest in something and get more out of it that your initial investment. The goal is a substantial return on investment. Whatever it takes, pay money and get financially invested in your transformation. Again, it is critical to invest by paying your hard-earned money for something.

It represents your personal involvement. Even if they are offered to you, do not accept gifts, because this is personal.

The money motivation is often referred to regarding a person's drive to earn money. Ironically, there is an increased motivation to avoid losing the money that was earned. Again, consider the person committed to a healthier lifestyle saying "I'm going to make green smoothies, my own dressings, and power shakes, and blend everything in sight, simply because I want to get use out of this expensive blender. I am going to go to the gym so I can wear my new training gear. I'm going to join Weight Watchers to ensure my food choices have been made, simply to show my full commitment to my desired transformative change." You may find that when you make such a commitment, others may offer support. In some cases, they may offer some of these items as gifts to you. Unfortunately, you must respectfully refuse to accept them and pay your hard-earned money for them, because it's personal.

This is just one of a host of different examples. The guiding factors are the financial commitment and the utility maximization principle. At one time in your life, you may have had the experience of ordering a meal that, once you began eating it, fell short of your expectations. It would seem logical that one would not eat something they do not enjoy. Ironically, with yourself and like many others, the tendency has been to finish the meal, if it is known that complaining will not result in a refund or complementary substitution. Barring starvation, the reason this meal is consumed is because a person does not want to feel as if they have totally wasted their money. How interesting is it that one will eat something that is not necessarily delightful, simply because they refuse to waste their money? They want to maximize their utility.

Money, or the commitment of money, has the ability to influence behavior. Get invested financially to your transformative change, and leverage the commitment of money to influence your behavior to align with your goal.

Money is void of an inherent value; it only possesses the value prescribed by the one who gives it and the one who accepts it.

UNKNOWN

Flood the Mind

THINKING ON PAPER

How do you plan on flooding the mind?

_____

_____

_____

_____

_____

What books, magazines, empowering contemporary electronic media resources, and enriching conversations do you plan on exposing yourself to in an effort to provide food for thought relative to your desired change?

_____

_____

_____

_____

_____

_____

_____

_____

_____

_____

_____

_____

_____

_____

_____

STEP 5

Flood the Mind

A man's mind may be likened to a garden, which may be intelligently cultivated or allowed to run wild; but whether cultivated or neglected, it must, and will, bring forth. If no useful seeds are put into it, then an abundance of useless weed seeds will fall therein, and will continue to produce their kind. Just as a gardener cultivates his plot, keeping it free from weeds and growing the flowers and fruits which he requires, so may a man tend the garden of his mind, weeding out all the wrong, useless, and impure thoughts and cultivating toward perfection the flowers and fruits of right, useful, and pure thoughts. By pursuing this process, a man sooner or later discovers that he is the master gardener of his soul, the director of his life. He also reveals within himself, the laws of thought, and understands with ever-increasing accuracy how the thought forces and mind elements operate in the shaping of his character, circumstances, and destiny.

—JAMES ALLEN

Another step in this process of transformation is going to be the action of flooding the mind. Once you have begun the process of transformative change, it is going to be essential that you leverage the use of your mind, especially the subconscious mind. When considering the mind, one may refer to the pathways of entry as the gates. Your eyes (what you see), your ears (what you hear), and your mouth (what you say) are all going to be critical influences on the mind.

In this day of technological advancement, your mind is subjected to the bombardment of a plethora of information. It can be a full-time job to simply protect your mind from all of the garbage that it is exposed to. The writer makes this reality very clear when he beseeches us to "guard your heart above all else, for it determines the course of your life" (Proverbs 4:23, NLT). A guard has the primary responsibility of protecting, and has been given the authority to permit and deny entrance. As we can see, the material manifestation of our life experiences germinates from the seeds sown into the heart—or, for our discussion, the mind. What you permit to enter your mind in abundance will sneak into your subconscious and manifest in your life. This may not always be a negative experience. When embarking on the journey to transformative change, the mind will play a critical role; therefore, what enters the mind will be regarded as a critical component. As we examine how the mind can be leveraged to assist us in achieving our goal of transformation consider the Law of Displacement.

As we have stated, information is always flowing, whether it be commercial marketing and advertising, music, television, the newspaper, the Internet, telephone apps, reading materials, school work, professional studies—the the list can go on, and change according to the current times. Consider a river flowing; it will most likely be impossible to completely stop the river from flowing, so the next logical option is to relocate from its pathway. When you relocate, you must consider the distance, because you also understand that there are some essentials you will need from the river. As you resettle, you now have the task of digging canals or constructing aqueducts that permit a controllable flow to your location.

In this task of transformative change, we must relocate from the uncontrollable bombardment of information and settle in a place where our contact with it is limited and controlled. The construction of mental aqueducts and canals will permit the filtration and purification process, and as a result, the flow will be less powerful and less violent. As the mental filtration and purification occurs, only the useful and constructive information should be permitted into the mind. Will some particles slip through the filter? Absolutely; however, their impact will be small, because of the one-sided ratio. As you begin this process, the Law of Displacement will be critical during the first phase. The mind has been subjected to years of information overload. Our current experiences are largely the result of what has been planted in our minds, and continue to remain there in abundance. The process of transformative change will require a deliberate and intentional channeling of specific information, relative and supportive to the change and new mindset you desire to establish. As you now bombard and flood the mind with the information that encourages, empowers, and establishes the foundation for your new thought process, the unproductive and destructive information that promotes undesired thoughts and conditions will be displaced. The time required for this process will depend on how much of the old has to be displaced. The purification and displacement process is critical, because the transformation must begin on the inside. To neglect the internal element and simply focus on the external garments of the change is to wear the costume of the one whom you would like to become without having the heartbeat that gives true life to the new being. Both are necessary. If you recall the account of Creation as recorded in the book of Genesis of the Holy Writ, the physical outer garments of man were created, and the appearance of man existed; however, man did not have true life until the breath of life was breathed into him. True transformation will require that breath of life, inspired by the internal change of a new thought process. I believe that as a man/woman thinks, so he/she becomes, and as he/she continues to think, so he/she remains. Establishing a new thought process will be achieved by flooding the mind and displacing the old, disempowering thoughts with the new, invigorating, and empowering thoughts. The mind must be reset to support the sustained transformation of the new you. This new mindset, which will influence your thoughts, will ultimately direct your actions—first on the conscious level, and eventually, if consistent, on a subconscious level. These new thoughts and actions will be the result of the deliberate and intentional filtration of information permitted to enter the mind. To your advantage, the outcome will be a true support for achieving and sustaining the transformation you desire.

As you reflect, consider that one of the first steps toward transformation will be to make a commitment to reading. Whatever transformation you would like to experience, begin to read, research, and study about it as a part of your commitment to expanding your knowledge base and familiarity. You should become so engaged and diligent in this process that you gradually become akin to a self-proclaimed expert on the subject. Flooding the mind is strategic and intentional. For example, if you were planning to go on a trip to an unfamiliar venue, you might attempt to learn as much as possible about the anticipated destination before you get there.

We now have a plethora of technologies that can assist in the process of flooding the mind. Our eyes and ears never have to lack visual or auditory stimuli; electronic and social media can almost guarantee that. Therefore, the availability—and in many cases, the cost-effectiveness—of these resources can be leveraged to support this objective. Use these platforms and tools to bombard and flood your eyes and ears with anything that supports the transformation you would like to see. Yes, make a "vision board," whether it is virtual or physical; leverage the use of imagery. Images are like pictures that get stapled or nailed to the wall of the mind, like a blueprint prepared by a creative architect awaiting the skilled craftsmanship of a confident builder. Once the images are posted, the mind engages in the process of manufacturing and constructing this blueprint into reality. The reinforcement will be your speech. What you speak about is critical as well; just as man was given life by the breath of the Creator, so will your transformation be given life by the words that you choose to speak into it. Positive and empowering words are words of life to your transformation, and anything else is counterproductive. You have to flood the mind. As you remain diligent in this process, you will notice that initially, most of the new information will be filtered and rejected by the conscious mind. However, as the process continues and the bombardment remains consistent, soon the overflow will begin to penetrate into the subconscious, resulting in your actions becoming automatic.

Once again, as a reminder, this effort must be a diligent and consistent one. Initially, the conscious mind will not work for you. It will serve as a guard that refuses to permit entry of this new information. It will diligently protect the status quo of your conditioned mindset. It will make every effort to block, divert, and weed out this new, contradictory information. To break past this barrier, you will have to breach your own mental levees. The Law of Intrusion must be employed. This law is built on the premise that small, incremental, and subtle changes, when consistent and deliberate, will change the physical or mental condition of a host.

In warfare, this principle refers to the fact that permitting one intruder into a territory changes the physical makeup of the territory. If a consistent effort is sustained, and the attrition is manageable, then in time, the establishment of an internal and external stronghold will make surrendering of the infiltrated unavoidable.

Just consider the ant you spot in your home. Understanding the behavioral and cultural characteristics of ants, you are fully aware that this single ant is most likely not traveling alone. As you spot another, then another, you probably begin your campaign to search diligently to locate their point of entry. This effort is motivated by your refusal to permit them taking over your home or establishing a foothold in it. You realize that every one that enters changes the living conditions of your home. If allowed, their colony can soon take residence. As we know, you will make great efforts to prevent this. However, the reality is that even if you killed many of them, if they just keep coming and finding different ways to enter, your efforts will soon be stifled. Your conscious mind will have the same fate. Your relentless and diligent effort to flood the mind will result in this new information slipping past the guard. Soon, the conscious mind will be bull-rushed, and the flooding of this new information will begin to displace and force out the roots of the old mindset. As your mind has suffered a hostile takeover, the conscious mind, after surrendering, is recruited and will begin to serve you rather than oppose the change. It is now on your team. As the conscious mind begins to block entry of the old mindset from returning, the second level of infiltration begins and the invasion of the subconscious ensues. Consistency and diligent, deliberate effort is key. Just think of the pixels on a screen. If we were to slow down the process, we would see that the transformation of the image we see is the result of millions of little pixels invading an existing image until all of the current pixels are replaced with the new ones, ultimately resulting in a new image—a total transformation.

Transformative Change is a Process and Also a Destination

Transforming is the process of being transformed. Since you have clearly defined what the transformative change will be, you can begin to renew the mind to think on the level of where you are going, rather than continuing to reinforce the mindset of where you are leaving.

In an earlier section, an analogy of a vacation was provided. This may be a bit misleading, because when one goes on vacation, one's learning is for a temporary stay, with the intention to return back to the original place of departure. On the other hand, if you are moving to another country, it may serve you well to begin to learn as much as possible before you arrive there. However, your learning is to prepare for a transition that has the objective of permanent residency. This preparation is because there is no intention to return to the original place of departure. You often hear "When in Rome, do as the Romans do." Let us consider the following: "Before moving to Rome, consider how the Romans think, observe how the Romans act, and learn what the Romans believe." Remember that you are not visiting; you are taking permanent residence. Transforming is your flight to Rome; transformation is your arrival in the city. When you have successfully completed the process of transformation, there is no turning back. You are a new person—an individual that has never existed before. Therefore, learn about where you are going—about who you are becoming—and renew your mind so that the change is not only external, but internal as well. This new person who you have become is ready and equipped to live in this new dimension.

Whatever we plant in our subconscious mind and nourish with repetition and emotion will one day become a reality.

⚠ WARNING

Please be warned that proceeding to this next section will require some very serious, and in some cases, difficult reflections and decisions. If you are not ready to embark on the tough choices that will involve seriously evaluating your current relationships and associations, then please refrain from proceeding and postpone this activity until you are mentally and emotionally ready. Please also be warned that you may never be mentally and emotionally ready. Pruning may be discomforting, but ultimately it promotes necessary growth.

Reestablish Your
Spheres of Influence

THINKING ON PAPER

CURRENT SPHERES

List the people you consider to occupy your *inner* circle (those close to you, and with whom you have frequent contact).

_____

_____

_____

_____

_____

_____

_____

_____

List the people you consider to occupy your *outer* circle (those that you have significant exposure and contact with, but the relationship is superficial and you can separate or dissociate from them with ease).

_____

_____

_____

_____

_____

_____

_____

_____

List the people you consider to occupy your peripheral circle (those whom you encounter from time to time, but who have little impact on your daily activities).

_____

_____

_____

_____

_____

_____

_____

_____

_____

_____

CONDUCT THE RELATIONSHIP AUDIT

Of your inner and outer circles (those whom you have the most contact and association with), place the people in the appropriate category, considering their dominant characteristic relative to their relationship with you. (For example, if Cousin Joe is your mentor in the business you run, then his dominant characteristic would be his experience and insight, therefore placing him in the Asset classification. On the other hand, if Amy is your co-worker and she takes up your entire lunch break informing you of the latest company gossip, then her dominant characteristic would be gossiper, unfortunately classifying her as a Liability.)

Relationship Audit

Asset	*Liability*

For each person listed on the classification table, describe the Asset value they add to your life or the Liability position they hold. (Be honest and forthright. This may take a little time to complete and may be somewhat uncomfortable.)

Name: _____

Relationship: _____

Asset or Liability

Explanation of specific Asset value or Liability position:

_____

_____

_____

_____

_____

Name: _____

Relationship: _____

Asset or Liability

Explanation of specific Asset value or Liability position:

_____

_____

_____

_____

_____

Name:

Relationship:

Asset or Liability

Explanation of specific Asset value or Liability position:

YOUR RE-ESTABLISHED SPHERE

- You will now only have two spheres: your inner circle and your peripheral circle.
- You must now re-establish your inner circle to include only those who have been labeled as assets. Everyone else must be relocated to the peripheral circle at minimum until the transformative change has been achieved. Whether they return later is totally up to you.

The Circle of Accountability

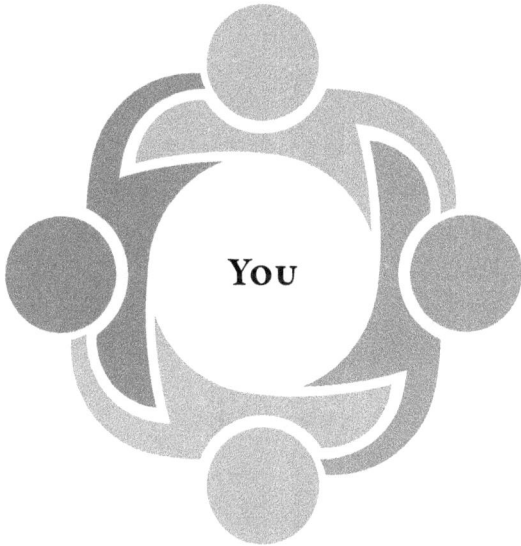

The Chief Accountability Officer (C.A.O.)

This person has free rein to keep you on track by any means necessary. Please be reminded that this person is not your "yes man" or "yes woman" or your cheerleader, but the one who will get in your face and hold you accountable.

Name _____

Why? _____

_____

_____

_____

Support Team Members:

_____

_____

_____

These people will hold you accountable also; however, they may be permitted to offer soft support and encouragement—but they can never accept excuses from you.

Critics and Naysayers:

_____

_____

_____

Please remember that these are not bad people. They simply do not take you seriously or believe that you can achieve your goal. They are free moral agents, and they have a right to doubt you if they so desire. It is your responsibility to monitor, ration, and strategically leverage your exposure to them.

STEP 6

Re-establish Your Spheres of Influence

The key is to keep company only with people who uplift you, whose presence calls forth your best.

—Epictetus

After flooding your mind, or while in the process of flooding your mind, you are allowing yourself to stay updated with relevant information pertaining to the transformation that you would like to experience. This next phase is going to be very important. This is such a critical phase that it could actually mean the difference between success and failure.

The next critical action you must take is to re-establish your spheres of influence. When we use the term "spheres of influence", we are referring to those around you that have an impact on your life. Undoubtedly, you know that your family is going to be essential; then consider your friends and your associates. They all make up your spheres of influence. If they have become a negative influence or impediment (specifically as pertaining to your goal of transformation), then they, unfortunately, must move or be pushed to the external sphere. This can definitely be conducted with tact and courtesy, and without a loss of love or significance. Your spheres of influence are going to be critical, because they will support the achievement of your transformation. Anything or anyone that does not support the achievement of your transformation must be removed or relocated. Remember, one of the most important things you will do in life is establish your core values and maintain healthy spheres of influence.

Consider evaluating the occupants of these spheres in economic terms. Referring to your inner circle, which is the most critical and influential sphere, the first question is: Is this relationship an asset or a liability? The asset value of a relationship is going to be based on conducting an authentic appraisal, and truthfully determining what is being added to your life by maintaining a relationship with this person. It may seem a little shallow, as if you are being overcritical, but it is very essential to your transformative change. Determine if this relationship is an asset or a liability. If it is not adding value, then it is actually taking value away, because all relationships require the investment of emotional energy. When you are embarking on a journey of transformative change, you must channel every bit of energy toward the achievement of this objective. Yes, family, friends, and associates will have to begin to be reassessed and relocated to their greatest contributing and least damaging positions.

Conducting the Relationship Audit

Regarding some difficult task, you may often hear an individual say "It's easier said than done." When it comes to the relationship audit, the truth of this phrase will be very evident. In life, we develop relationships as we navigate through different seasons and times. These relationships take on different forms and serve different purposes, in addition to maintaining varying depths and time-frames. As we progress through life, a good practice is to take inventory of these relationships, and evaluate them based on the season and time we are navigating through. Unfortunately, you will not have the luxury of an accountant to move allocations and expenditures on a spreadsheet. This process will directly involve people whom you may be very close to: acquaintances, friends, and even adversaries. You and the accountant may deal with different elements; however, the process is similar and the criteria is universal. You have the daunting task and critical responsibility of removing that which no longer serves you. In this particular case, it will be evaluating your relationships and making tough but necessary decisions. Unlike the accountant, it is not just business; for you, it is also business but also very personal.

Before You Grab the Pen

1. Take a moment to reflect

2. Understand that you are not a bad person for what you are about to do

3. Keep the vision at the forefront of your thinking, and know the "why" for your transformation

IDENTIFYING POSITIVE PEOPLE

1. Are they positive and supportive?
2. Do they themselves have vision?
3. Do they inspire you?

IDENTIFYING "DIFFERENT" PEOPLE

People have the right to be different, and you have no right to judge them. However, you can respect them, but you are not obligated to embrace them. We regard these people as different because they simply differ from the type of people that you will allow in your sphere of influence as you embark on your journey of transformation.

THE USE OF SCHEMAS

Schemas are sets of cognitions that are used as a way to assist us in categorizing experiences. Consequently, they are also the foundation of preconceptions, prejudice, and judgments. In this context, however, establishing schemas will assist in categorizing the "different" people so that our encounters, interactions, and experiences are strategic, but also informed. When people are identified, unrealistic expectations can be eliminated. They are accepted for who they are, and their positioning in your life is more strategic and deliberate. In some cases, your contact cannot be avoided, and therefore your interactions must be managed. Again, you are not to judge them, but judge the relationship and how it serves your growth and progression towards your goal of transformation. These people, regardless of their intentions, tend to bring an aura of negativity. They may say negative things about you, which can ultimately have an impact on your self-esteem, self-perception, and self-efficacy. This is simply too critical to be left unaddressed. Again, if contact and communication cannot be eliminated, it must be managed. More importantly, your perspective must be adjusted. This will make all the difference. Of the many interactions with people you encounter on a daily basis, the different people will fall into one of three categories (schemas): The Ignorant, the Misinformed, and the Liars.

HOW TO EVALUATE THE "DIFFERENT" PEOPLE

1. Listen to their speech
2. Observe their actions
3. Acknowledge how they think (their perspective)

Remember, your evaluation is focused primarily on their interactions with you.

As you know, this audit can be one of the most difficult

things you have to do in life; however, it also is probably one of the most important. Some people are so damaging and destructive to your life that you may have to issue a mental order of protection against them. Removing them from your life is obvious, and sometimes it is easier to do because their negative impact is evident. Protect your sanity and your peace. Place your security guards on the borders so that they can spot these intruders trying to re-enter. You must employ spiritual sharpshooters so that if negativity attempts to invade your inner circle, it can be dealt with immediately. Those spiritual sharpshooters are looking out for disturbances or impediments to your goal. The value of your life and the goals you aspire to must be important enough to you to support their attainment.

The real challenge is when a counterproductive relationship or association is not so obvious. In many cases, people pursue goals that will benefit not only themselves, but also those they care about most. Your change may require a vacation or sabbatical from anything or anyone that does not fully align with the attainment of your transformation—even good people. Please be reminded that you are not excommunicating these people, but in some cases, you must establish that you will only have limited contact with them.

Apologize, Then Do What is Necessary

Proximity—not simply referring to physical space, but influential significance as well—is another critical consideration. Certain "well-meaning" people will have to be relocated temporarily from your inner circle. Most importantly, those are the people who have grown to accept you for who you are. It is often the case that those who accept you for who you are will be the ones who may reject who you want to become.

We all have been taught, or at least told at one point in our lives, that we need to accept people for who they are. This seems ideal; however, when it relates to transformative change, this ideology can be detrimental to your progression. Such people are great for society, but can be a major hindrance to your transformative change. Just think: You have decided that you want to change, that you are no longer willing to accept who you are, in order to pursue the person you would like to become. Therefore, those in your inner sphere should no longer accept who you are. They must encourage and support your pursuit of transformation, and make the unchanged version of yourself very uncomfortable. Unfortunately, it is often the case that well-meaning people who know you, and who may be very happy that you would like to change, may at the same time assure you that "We love you regardless." They may accept the intention and the effort, but fail to hold you accountable for the anticipated result. They may say, "Don't worry; at least you tried," or, "What you are trying to do is difficult, and you know you don't have to do this. We love you just the way you are." They want to provide you with comfort and acceptance. They want to remove as much social pressure as possible. This, unfortunately, establishes a comfortable safe haven for the status quo of mediocrity and failure. Once you have decided who you want to become, then you need people around you that make it uncomfortable for who you currently are.

It would be a disservice to present this as if it were an easy task. Just think: Most of your close friends have grown accustomed to who you are. This "new" person may not be so welcomed in their circle. The new, transformed you may be treated with animosity and resentment. Leaving the pack has its social consequences; however, it also has its rewards. When you are embarking on a transformative change, you may lose some close friends and associates. They may say, "You have been acting different," or "Something has changed about you." Deep down in your heart, you may be rejoicing that such an acknowledgement is confirmation that the transformation is noticeable and evident; but externally, you may seek to save the relationship and sacrifice your efforts and progress by changing your behavior to maintain acceptance—a tough decision, but a real one. The reality is that you are not "acting" different; you are different. The butterfly has wings; the caterpillar has potential for wings. The reality is that one can fly, and the other cannot. The process is known to both: one from having gone through it, and the other from having heard about it. Should the butterfly sacrifice its wings to make the caterpillar comfortable? Should the caterpillar go through the process to obtain its wings to fly with the butterfly? Or should they just accept the reality that they are now different, and go their separate ways?

Consider your true friends and those who really care about you. When you embark on this journey of transformation, they will either run alongside of you or stand along the side and cheer you on. These people will support you from wherever they can. Those who do not will fade out of your life, and that is okay also. They most likely would not be able to deal with the transformed you, anyway. There does not need to be any hard feelings. This is just a time in your life where you have approached a fork in the road. You have chosen to go in one direction, and they have chosen to go in another. Maybe you will meet up again on life's path, or maybe you will not. Consider the game of life: You are in the game as a player. There are different levels of contact to people, based on their positioning. The closest are those in the game with you; they have direct contact. Then you have those on the sideline; you may hear their voices, but you must remain focused on the game while knowing that they are supporting you and desire your success. Then you have those who have good seats; you can see them if you look, and may hear them if they are loud; however, your communication with them is usually limited to long time-outs or breaks in the game. They seem to support you also, but may not fully understand the game you are in. Yes, they mean well; but contact is limited because of this lack of understanding. They will cheer for the good plays, but may boo for some of the mistakes that will be made. You understand that good decisions and mistakes are both are a part of the game, but they may not. Then you have those in the upper level; they are there just for the excitement. You know that they are there because they always show up; however, you cannot see them. You may have contact with them before you enter the arena. After that, there is a slim possibility that you may see them again when the game is over, either to praise you for victory or heckle you for defeat. In many cases, you will not see them at all, because they will most likely leave after the initial excitement fades. When they cheer or boo, you cannot hear them because they are so far away. In life, these people, if they stay and support you, may get better seats next time; and if they leave, you are thankful for the time they did spend in your life. Everyone has a role in your life; however, you determine their significance.

SUPPORT NETWORKS

It is very important to establish strategic support networks. These support networks are people and relationships that you establish around yourself to support the achievement of your desired transformation. Everyone else must be relocated to the exterior. This is essential. The challenge we have identified will be the reality that you may have to come to terms with yourself, and acknowledge that people with whom you have had long-lasting relationships are now a liability that is too great for you to assume. Because you have determined the transformative change to be of necessity in your life, anything or anyone that does not support it must be removed; so these spheres of influence are going to be important, because every relationship will have an effect. Regardless of how pronounced the contact may seem, there will be an exchange of energy that takes place.

One may inquire why so much emphasis is placed on the reestablishing of these spheres of influence. Consider a marathon runner and a sprinter: Neither would benefit from carrying additional weight. Both understand that the action of sprinting or running distance will be challenging enough without anything else weighing them down or holding them back. The resistance is for training purposes, to make the individual stronger; however, when the training is over, the resistance is removed. If certain people are not supporting the achievement of your transformation, then they must be moved to the exterior and they must stay there. You must limit your contact with these individuals, because they do not assist in or support your transformation. An asset adds value, and a liability maintains an inherent cost. Consequently, these support networks will be critical, and you must identify and establish them immediately. Your support network at the beginning may be very small, because of the limited number of people that may believe in your vision for transformation. Over time, however, this network may grow to include people you may never have considered. Regardless, throughout the process, your goal of transformation must remain the focus.

The Circle of Accountability

Another critical circle that you must establish is an accountability circle. These are people who are not afraid to confront you when you are taking steps in the wrong direction, as it pertains to the specific transformative change that you have articulated. These people are people that you are going to employ to get in your face and tell you when you are straying, or when your actions are inconsistent with the transformative change you would like to see. These individuals may not always be friends or family; they may be people that actually take pleasure in confronting you. On this journey, you really cannot afford to have everyone say "Oh, everything is going to be okay. It's no problem." If you are not following through with your steps to transformation, it is not okay, and there is a problem with your actions or inaction. When appropriate and necessary, you want these people to say, "You know, it is pathetic that you have strayed this far from your goal. Let's go. Pick yourself up and get back on track!"

Consider the Chief Accountability Officer (CAO). You must find someone that is not afraid to get in your face and tell you that you are not doing what you are supposed to be doing. You must find someone that cares more about you than your feelings. This person is very critical, because when they are put in a position to choose between you and your feelings, they must refuse to compromise and choose you—referring to your articulated goal—in every case. Unfortunately for you, it will require thick skin. This person will be granted the green light to speak openly and honestly. Once they know your intended transformation, they must have no reservations or apprehensions in calling you out. If you are slacking, they will call you out; if you are making excuses, they will call you out. Even if you are legitimately having a difficult time, they will leverage their personality trait of being extremely inconsiderate to the feelings of others, and tell you to suck it up and get back in the game. They must refuse to accept any excuse whatsoever. They will maintain a "shut up and get it done" relationship with you. Because of the potential of this relationship to become hostile, it may be wise to outsource such aggression. This person should not be required to have tact, good human relationship skills, or a whole lot of compassion. Your transformation and the steps and efforts necessary to achieve it are their only concerns. Everything else is irrelevant to them. Therefore, if you choose a friend, be forewarned that the relationship will be tested and possibly compromised; the person you choose to serve this role has one focus, and that is your transformation. Keep this person close, regardless of how much you may grow to hate them. Respect their role in your life during this time.

This person, and the people like them that you recruit, are going to be assets to you because they are going to be like those bumpers that will not go away. They will not embrace you when you crawl to the sideline of life, with the intention of quitting and settling for less than what you desired. You will not hear them say, "Don't worry about it; at least you tried." These people are going to be those bumpers that push back hard, refusing to allow you to quit, give up, or settle. They will push you back on track leaving you no option but to fight and continue towards your goals. They will not allow you to accept the excuses that you make for yourself and may possibly make you uncomfortable, and even be considered annoying. Some may be outright disrespectful and inconsiderate. So what? Deal with it! You may hate them now, but you will undoubtedly thank them later. They are your circle of accountability. Remove the comfort, and do not under any circumstance put people in your circle of accountability that are too close to you to confront you. It is for your own good. This circle of accountability has to be like a low-voltage electrical fence: If you bump into them, you will be shocked, but you will not die. The shock is an indication that you have strayed a little too far, and you need to get back on track. Again, the importance of a strong accountability circle cannot be neglected.

THE CIRCLE OF CRITICS AND NAYSAYERS

Consider this next group of people: your critics and naysayers. Their intention is irrelevant; however, their actions will serve as fuel for your motivation. Believe it or not, they will be leveraged to actually propel you; however, please be warned that despite the importance of these people and the establishment of this circle, it will be critical that you have reached a certain level of maturity before you can employ or leverage their dispositions. At a certain point in your journey, you are going to strategically leverage some of the doubters, critics, and overly judgmental people that were moved to the outer spheres of your life. When you have matured, you will recruit them for a specific purpose that they may be totally unaware of. You will use their negativity as motivation. It will be those people that you know are naysayers—the ones that, when you communicate to them the transformative change you would like to see, you know deep down in your heart are going to laugh at you, the ones you know are going to say, "Yeah, right; that will never happen." They are not going to believe you. This is good, because it's going to allow you to build those inner muscles that will support you to believe in yourself. They will help train you to say, "I know I can, and I will" in the face of challenges and opposition.

These negative people in your life will now serve a purpose to motivate you. You do not always need someone to say, "I know you can do it; just stay focused and put your mind to it." Sometimes you need people in your life to tell you, "You can't do it." A person that is truly committed to their transformative change says in their heart, "You tell me I can't, but I say 'Watch me.'" This builds character and an inner confidence that says, "Everyone may not support me, but I support myself. Everyone may not believe in me, but I believe in myself." This is critical, because you want that negativity to be fuel for your engine, to motivate you to say "I will do it in spite of nobody believing in me." When you achieve your goal, the transformative change is going to be for your betterment, not theirs. Therefore, their negativity can be fuel in the engine of your motivation.

Leveraging these people is important; however, what is even more critical is that you encounter these people in prescribed, strategic, and limited doses. You have to know how much you can take. Just like when you are working out, use just enough weight to get the job done—too much and you can get hurt, too little and you waste your time and energy. Know when they have served their purpose and then relocate them back to the outer spheres, because if you start to believe what they say, it becomes counterproductive. Basically, rack your weights after you are finished using them.

The importance of your strategic spheres of influence cannot be emphasized enough. Whether it is life in general, or a specific transformative change, these spheres are made of people and relationships that all play a role. You are encouraged to reexamine your social portfolio and emotional balance sheet. Evaluate your relationships and associations and determine their true worth. Which ones are currently assets, and which are currently liabilities? Then look at where your emotional energy and social involvement are being invested. Only you can provide a true and authentic appraisal, and only you can make the necessary adjustments. Your life is like a beautiful edifice for which you are the architect, the builder, and the occupant. You must design it with intention, and you must build it with precision, so that you may enjoy the comfort and beauty that your commitment and labor has produced.

Surround yourself with good people—people who are going to be honest with you and look out for your best interests.

–DEREK JETER

REFLECTION NOTES:

REFLECTION NOTES:

REFLECTION NOTES:

REFLECTION NOTES:

REFLECTION NOTES:

www.ingramcontent.com/pod-product-compliance
Lightning Source LLC
Chambersburg PA
CBHW072206090426
42740CB00012B/2412